molly Hanson

C000245218

V

Free Fall

Bloomsbury Methuen Drama
An imprint of Bloomsbury Publishing Plc

B L O O M S B U R Y
LONDON · NEW DELHI · NEW YORK · SYDNEY

Bloomsbury Methuen Drama

An imprint of Bloomsbury Publishing Plc

Imprint previously known as Methuen Drama

50 Bedford Square	1385 Broadway
London	New York
WC1B 3DP	NY 10018
UK	USA

www.bloomsbury.com

BLOOMSBURY, METHUEN DRAMA and the Diana logo
are trademarks of Bloomsbury Publishing Plc

This playtext first published by Bloomsbury Methuen Drama 2014

Script © Vinay Patel 2014

Vinay Patel has asserted his right under the Copyright, Designs
and Patents Act 1988 to be identified as the author of this work.

British Library Cataloguing-in-Publication Data
A catalogue record for this book is available from the British Library

ISBN: PB: 978-1-4742-3422-1
ePDF: 978-1-4742-3424-5
ePub: 978-1-4742-3421-4

Library of Congress Cataloging-in-Publication Data
A catalog record for this book is available from the Library of Congress

Series: Modern Plays

Typeset by Country Setting, Kingsdown, Kent CT14 8ES
Printed and bound in Great Britain

Poleroid Theatre presents

FREE FALL

by Vinay Patel

The first performance of this production
was at Pleasance Theatre, Islington,
on 14 October 2014

FREE FALL

by Vinay Patel

Cast

Roland	Maynard Eziashi
Andrea	Molly Roberts

Director	Bethany Pitts
Designer	Petra Hjortsberg
Producer	Chris Snow
Sound and Music	Jon McLeod
Lighting Designer	Ben Jacobs
Production/Stage Manager	Katie Jackson
Fight Choreography	Phil Dunster
Dialect Coach	Emma Roberts
Assistant Producer	Hannah Groombridge

PR	Laura Horton
Marketing	Boris Van Der Ree
Photography	Chris Mann
	Richard Davenport
Graphic Design	Rebecca Pitt

Proudly supporting
HLC Dartford and DGS Mind

Special Thanks

Alex Hylands-White, Anna Brewer, Bransby Roberts,
Charles Smith, Chris Hislop, David Cockney, David Nolan,
David Sanders, Elspeth Morrison, Emma Craft, Farokh Soltani,
Finn Anderson, Francesca Clarke, Graeme Thompson,
Greg Bernstein, IdeasTap, Imogen Sarre, Jack Pirie, Jackson Ingle,
James Rose, James Tupper, Jamie Gibbard, Jean Diamond,
Jen Payne, Jennifer Havisham, Jocelyn Abbey, John O'Donovan,
Julie Roberts, Kanika Clayton, Kathy Noble, Katy Fattuhi,
Kelly Knatchbull, Kenny Emson, Kevin Mathurin, Laura Kenwright,
Liz Webster, Mark Lovell, Martin Cavannagh, Matt Bradford,
Matt King, Michael Lovelock, Mick Fox, Miranda Dodwell,
Neil Dowden, Paapa Essiedu, Peter de Silva, Rachel Crowther,
Rebecca Hill, Richard Giles, Rowan Ilsley, Sarah French,
Sarah Loader, Sharon Phillips, Sophia Simensky, Steven Flynn,
Tania Hurst-Brown, The Camden Collective, Toby Roberts,
Tim Williams, Tom Clancy

Photo: Chris Mann

Vinay Patel | Playwright

Vinay studied for an MA in Writing for Stage and Broadcast Media at the Royal Central School of Speech and Drama, graduating with distinction in 2011. Since then, he has won competitions run by Ideastap, the BBC, the National Youth Theatre, Shine Drama and the Brockley Jack Studio Theatre, and made the top 5 per cent of the BBC Writersroom 2013 intake with his radio play *Twenty Million Shirts*. His short plays have been produced at Bush Theatre, Theatre503 and Park Theatre among others. His debut full-length play, *True Brits* – written as part of his attachment to HighTide Festival Theatre and published by Methuen Drama – premiered at Assembly Hall, Edinburgh Fringe, 2014 before transferring to the Bush Theatre as part of the 2014 RADAR Festival. He is currently developing projects for the BBC and Channel 4 as well as an historical political thriller, *Sons of India*, about the relationship between Mahatma Gandhi and Subhas Chandra Bose.

Maynard Eziashi | Roland

Maynard has over 25 years experience as a professional actor, and won the Silver Bear Award for Best Actor at the 41st Berlin International Film Festival in 1991 for *Mister Johnson*, starring alongside Pierce Brosnan. Other film credits include *The Contract*, *Kiss Kiss Bang Bang*, *When Brendan Met Trudy*, *Ace Ventura: When Nature Calls*, *A Good Man in Africa*, *Bopha* and *Twenty-One*. Television includes *Casualty*, *Hotel Babylon*, *The Changeling* and *The Bill*. Theatre includes *The Dead Wait* (Park Theatre), *Wedlock of the Gods* (Cochrane Theatre), *Faith V Reason* (Bush Theatre), *The Winter's Tale* (RSC), *Pericles* (RSC), *Guess Who's Coming for Dinner* (St Andrew's Lane Theatre, Dublin), *A Jamaican Airman Foresees His Death* (Royal Court) and *A Respectable Wedding* (Almeida Theatre). Maynard plays the recurring role of Charlie in BBC Radio 4's *The No. 1 Ladies' Detective Agency* series.

Molly Roberts | Andrea

Molly is an Acting graduate of the Guildford School of Acting and is Artistic Director/ Executive Producer for Poleroid Theatre.

Theatre includes *Life on a Plum* (Wilderness Festival), *The Allotment R&D* (Live Theatre), *Timebomb* (White Bear Theatre), *Our Father* (Theatre503), *Snow, At the End of the World* (Old Red Lion Theatre), *Me, as a Penguin* (Guildford Fringe), *Writers Bloc: WaterWings* (Old Red Lion Theatre), *Burn: Fahrenheit 451* (ELAN Frantoio, Italy), *Breakout* (Cockpit Theatre), *Dracula* (Broadway Theatre), *Back2Back* (White Bear Theatre), *FlickBook* (Theatre503) and *Shakers* (Mill Studio, Yvonne Arnaud Theatre). Molly is currently co-creating a new comedy series with Channel X TV Productions. She is also Associate Producer for Third Man Theatre and has Assistant Produced for nabokov.

Television includes *Inspector George Gently* (BBC), *Tony Robinson's Gods and Monsters* (Channel 4), *Flat 32* (Online Series/Channel X) and *Michelle and Michael* (Highsix Media).

www.molly-roberts.co.uk

Bethany Pitts | Director

Bethany is a theatre director specialising in new work, both scripted and devised, and has trained in directing with Katie Mitchell, Di Trevis, Lyndsey Turner, Told by an Idiot and through the Young Vic Directors Programme. She was Assistant Director at Theatre Royal Plymouth from 2012 to 2013, working under Artistic Director Simon Stokes, and prior to that worked as Resident Assistant Director at Theatre503. She co-runs the MolinoGroup for whom directing includes *DESERT* (national tour/Latitude Festival) and *The Roland Piece* (Bike Shed Theatre/Rosemary Branch Theatre). Freelance directing credits include *Spine* (Soho/Underbelly – Fringe First and Stage Award winner 2014), *Acres* (New Diorama), *The Caravan* (Park Theatre), *The Neighbour* (Arcola Theatre) and *Locked* (Ovalhouse), and assisting includes *Theatre Uncut* at the Young Vic, *Dark Vanilla Jungle* by Philip Ridley (Soho Theatre/Pleasance Theatre – Fringe First winner 2013), *Forever House* and *The Astronaut's Chair* by Rona Munro (The Drum, Theatre Royal Plymouth) and *Girl in the Yellow Dress* (Theatre503). She is also a freelance script reader for venues including The Drum and writing competitions including King's Cross New Writing Award.

Petra Hjortsberg | Designer

Petra is an award-nominated theatre and performance designer who works internationally across theatre, opera, dance and film. Most recent theatre design credits include the highly acclaimed *Freak* (Assembly Rooms/Theatre503) and the Offie Best Set Design nominated *Occupied* (Theatre503) as well as associate design credits on *Land of Our Fathers* and *A Handful of Stars* (Trafalgar Studios). Other theatre credits include *How to Win Against History* (Ovalhouse), *Companion Piece* (Pleasance Islington), *Treasure This?* (Bush Theatre), *In Extremis* (King's Head Theatre), *Cnoic Chlaonta* and *Shift(h)er* (USA and Ireland), *Celebrity* (Project Arts Centre, Dublin), *DISCOnnected* and the award-nominated *Body Electric* (ABSOLUT Fringe Festival, Dublin). Film and video credits include *Magpie*, *Way of the Monkey's Claw*, *The 95th*, *PubMonkey*, *Blind Man's Dream* and *Termination* as well as costume work for the UK artists Cloud Boat and Mila Falls. In 2013 Petra exhibited at the World Stage Design Exhibition. She is a Creative Associate at the Gate Theatre and Associate Artist with Baseless Fabric Theatre Company.

www.petrahjortsberg.com

Chris Snow | Producer

Chris runs FreeRange Productions, is Assistant Producer for Snapdragon Productions and Resident Producer at Poleroid Theatre. Credits as producer or associate include the 2014 Fringe First winning *Travesti* (Pleasance Dome), *Sex, with Benefits* (Sweet Venues), *The Dead Wait* (Park Theatre), *Shakespeare's Cymbeline* (The Caves), *This Was Your Life* (UK fringe tour), *Thark* (Park Theatre), *The Hound of the Baskervilles* (Reading Amphitheatre), *Montmorency* (C Venues), *The Three Faces of Doctor Crippen* (C Venues/Etcetera Theatre), *Bea* (South Street Arts Centre) and *Love Remains* (Leicester Square Theatre/South Hill Park).

www.chris-snow.co.uk

Jon McLeod | Sound and Music

Jon studied BA Sound Design at the Leeds College of Music and MA Advanced Theatre Practice at the Royal Central School of Speech and Drama. Credits include *A Conversation* and *Party Skills for the End of the World* (Nigel Barrett and Louise Mari), *In the Neuron Forest*, *Terminus Treats* and *The Eyes Have It* (Bread & Goose), *Spine* (Soho Theatre), *Square Bubble* (Watch This Space), *Nightmare Dreamer* and *Flying Roast Goose* (Blue Elephant Theatre), *The Fanny Hill Project* (Theatre State), *Borderline Vultures* (The Lowry), *66 Minutes in Damascus* (LIFT Festival) and *The Invisible Show* (Red Shift Theatre) as well as associate sound designer for *Damned by Despair* (National Theatre). His own play *Organs of Little Apparent Importance* was produced for HighTide Festival.

www.jonmcleod.com

Ben Jacobs | Lighting Designer

Ben is currently training in Lighting Design at the Royal Central School of Speech and Drama. Recent theatre lighting design credits include *The Greene Card* (The Space), *Fanny & Faggot* (Tabard Theatre), *4AM in the Middle of the Night* (Camden People's Theatre) and *The Improvised History of the World* (Tête à Tête Opera Festival). Recent assisting credits include *Jason and the Argonauts* (Courtyard Theatre), *Out of His Skin* (UK tour) and *Finding Joy* (UK tour).

Katie Jackson | Stage Manager

Katie graduated with a Foundation Degree in Technical Theatre and Stage Management from RADA. RADA credits include *The Sea* (director Edward Kemp) and *She Stoops to Conquer* (director Jonathan Miller) and work on five of the RADA short films. As part of her degree, Katie completed an eight-week Stage Management placement at Shakespeare's Globe Theatre working on a production of *The Merchant of Venice* (director Bill Buckhurst). Katie worked as venue crew for the Pleasance at the Edinburgh Fringe Festivals 2013 and 2014.

Hannah Groombridge | Assistant Producer

Hannah is an independent theatre producer. Having recently finished the Assistant Producer internship at the King's Head Theatre, her current producing credits include *The Picture of John Gray* at the Old Red Lion Theatre, *Margaret Thatcher Queen of Soho* at Edinburgh Fringe and *Rachel* at the Finborough Theatre. She is an alumnus of the Stage One New Producers Workshop.

Photo: Chris Mann

·PLEASANCE·

Pleasance Theatre, Islington

Pleasance Edinburgh opened as part of the 1985 Festival Fringe, and has gone on to become one of the biggest and most highly respected venues at the Edinburgh Festival Fringe.

The Pleasance Theatre Islington has been one of the most exciting Fringe theatres in London since it opened its doors in 1995, providing a launch pad for some of the most memorable productions and renowned practitioners of the past decade and staying true to its mission of providing a platform for the talent of the future.

Director	Anthony Alderson
General Manager	Hamish Morrow
Theatre Programmer	Matthew Dwyer
Head of Comedy	Ryan Taylor
Marketing Manager	Stuart Hurford
Edinburgh Operations Manager	Matt Britten
London Theatre Manager	Dan O'Neill
London Production Manager	Josephine Tremelling
Technical Manager	Andres Velasquez
Head of Finance	Yvonne Goddard
Box Office Manager	Chrissy Angus
Deputy Box Office Manager	Sam Smith
Front of House Manager	Dan Smiles
Admin and Finance Assistant	Jenny Halsey

HLC Dartford

The Healthy Living Centre Dartford is a friendly, community-led service. The aim of the centre is to promote healthy lifestyle choices in Dartford and surrounding areas through providing access to exercise and activity sessions, help to give up smoking, information and support to make healthy, positive choices for individuals and families, opportunities to volunteer and basic IT support sessions.

The Healthy Living Centre is based at St Edmund's Church Living Well in Temple Hill, Dartford.

www.hlcdartford.btck.co.uk

DGS Mind

DGS Mind is an independent mental health charity operating in North West Kent, providing a wide range of services for people who experience mental health problems. DGS Mind also provide supportive services for people who are the carers of those who experience these problems.

www.dgsmind.co.uk

Poleroid Theatre

Artistic Director/Executive Producer – **Molly Roberts**

Poleroid Theatre was founded in 2011 to discover and craft the contemporary image of young emerging artists in the UK and give new talent a platform through the creation of eclectic, fast-paced, immediate theatre.

Since forming, Poleroid have built a strong reputation for exposing emerging talent. Previous productions include *FlickBook* (Theatre503/ Etcetera), *Back2Back* (White Bear), *Breakout* (Cockpit), *Peanuts* (Tristan Bates/Last Refuge), *Instadate* (Hackney Attic/Ritzy Cinema), *Our Father* (Theatre503), *Timebomb* (White Bear); *WIMI: Look, This Is Your Life* (Wilderness Festival); *The Allotment R&D* (Live Theatre); *Write It: Mic It* (Hackney Attic/Manchester Castle Hotel/ Edinburgh Fringe).

Poleroid have worked with writers, directors, musicians and actors from a wide range of backgrounds including the Royal Court Young Writers Programme and Studio Group, Old Vic New Voices, Young Vic Directors Programme, Live Theatre Newcastle, BBC and a multitude of different drama schools.

Poleroid is generously supported by The Camden Collective.

Poleroid Theatre Ltd. is a registered limited company no 8337621.
hello@poleroidtheatre.co.uk

www.poleroidtheatre.co.uk

Free Fall

For Dartford
For Thurrock
For Mum

Characters

Andrea, *twenty-three, white, Essex*
Roland, *forty-seven, black, Kent*

Setting

The Queen Elizabeth II Bridge, Dartford, Kent.

Notes

A slash (/) signals an interruption from the other character.

Directions and inflections are merely suggestions. They are included to give an image of the play to the reader and may be edited or ignored by the director if they so wish.

Scene One

Half midnight. The Queen Elizabeth II Bridge. It's very dark.

Sound of an engine approaching, car headlights sweep across the stage. The engine stops.

Andrea *emerges from the black. She wears a thin coat with bulging pockets over a cardigan. A scarf is wrapped around her neck and the lower half of her face.*

In her fingers she twiddles with some stones. She rams them into the pockets.

She clambers on to the outermost girder of the bridge and clutches a support beam.

She takes a good look down.

Andrea (*muffled*)   Wowzer.

She lowers the scarf. A bruise sits proud on her cheek. She looks down again.

The enormity of what she's about to do dawns on her.

She hops up and down.

Right. OK. Alright.

She closes her eyes, takes a moment to herself, then shapes to jump. She halts. Second attempt, she begins swinging, building momentum, but again doesn't follow through.

Come on, come on, fucking . . . man up!

A third attempt. It looks as if she'll go this time, but she pulls back at the last minute and screams. She starts hitting herself repeatedly.

God Almighty, you useless piece of shit . . . !

She fumbles a mobile phone out of her coat, dials, and waits for an answer.

Hiya, it's me. Yeah, I know it's late, just thought I'd – no I ain't drunk. I haven't – I did a double shift. At *work*, Mum,

I went to work. No, I can't get you that, we don't do it, need to go to a pharmacy or –

She listens impatiently to the reply.

Mum, look, I don't give a toss about your haemorrhoids right now, sorry, can you just tell me, is he . . .

No, 's alright, figured he might be. Nah, nah, it's not important, don't wake him up, just tell him that I – hang on, I'm . . .

She checks the phone with incredulity.

Getting another call . . . ?

She switches calls.

'Allo? Oh, for crying out loud, I didn't steal your stapler! I didn't, I bloody didn't, but you can borrow mine, OK? In fact, you can have it, why not, bottom drawer. (*Under her breath.*) Fucking fuck 'tard.

Shuffling footsteps. **Roland** *approaches, undetected. He wears a suit with a bulky hi-vis jacket over it and is nonchalantly eating cashew nuts.*

Andrea *slumps down.*

Andrea   Shitting hell, Janet, obviously not *your* bottom drawer, why would it be in your bottom drawer, look in mine, it's there under the – No, no just do it, there's no point clearing it with Gary. Because two idiots combined will not a solution create. This really ain't the best time anyway, Janet, bit out the way at the minute, think I might lose . . .

She looks down.

. . . reception.

Roland   I doubt that.

Andrea   FUCK!

Surprised, she drops the phone. She's horrified.

Roland   Doubt that very much indeed, the signal's smashing out here, clear road from you to the heavens. Odd place for a call though, important was it?

He looks at where the phone fell.

(*Cheery.*) Not that that really matters any more.

Andrea   You made me drop my phone, you fucking dipshit!

Roland   Language, young lady.

Andrea   Seriously? The fuck do you want?

Roland   I'm the supervisor.

Andrea   So?

Roland   So this is my bridge, I'm responsible for what happens on it and this very much looks like something happening.

Andrea   Something that's nothing to do with you.

Roland   Fair play, just thought I'd bring you this.

He pulls a coin out for inspection. She squints at it.

Andrea   20p.

Roland   It's your change. For the toll, you overpaid. I see you were in a hurry.

He holds out the coin for her and takes a few steps forward.

Andrea   Oi!

She grabs a stone out of her pocket and raises it at him.

Keep back!

Roland *stops.* **Andrea** *glances out to the river.* **Roland** *starts to inch closer.* **Andrea** *notices.*

Andrea   We're not playing Grandmother's fucking Footsteps, mate! Stay away, or I'll jump!

He inches closer still.

Roland   Won't you jump anyway?

Andrea   Well . . . yeah.

Roland   So what's it matter if I –

He nudges forward again.

Andrea   I'm saying if you don't stay away, I'll jump *sooner*.

Roland   Jump off the bridge.

Andrea   Obviously.

Roland   To what end would that be, then? So it's accurate for my log.

Andrea   To what – what end do you reckon?

Roland   Need to be sure. I mean, I assume you're not out there to catch a tan off the street lamps, but you might have a bungee rope, we do get the odd bungeer around here, you might have a bungee rope hidden away there and –

Andrea   I'm going to drown myself. Happy?

Roland   Oh. Wow. In the Thames, huh?

He makes a face.

Andrea   What?

Roland   Just. I mean, hell, I don't know how clued up you are about water quality but to be honest, you might as well piss into a glass and choke on that.

Andrea   River's fine, thanks.

Roland   Just trying to help.

Andrea   Ain't nothing here for you to help with. This is happening, I am done.

She contemplates the water.

Roland (*with little enthusiasm*)   Surely there's something I can say to convince you to . . .

He looks for the right words.

(*Louder but again with little enthusiasm.*) You've probably got so much to live for?

She turns to him with a questioning look.

Andrea   You are fucking shite at this, you know that?

Roland   Look, to be honest, I don't actually mind you trying to kill yourself, free country and all that, but it'd just be a waste of everyone's morning.

Andrea   I'll try make it quick, should I?

Roland   It's not the *fall* time that concerns me – I mean, you look like you'd drop pretty fast, no, it's just that it's impossible.

Andrea   That right? And how'd you figure that, smart arse?

Roland   'Cause you'll never clear the nets.

Andrea (*aghast*)   Nets?! You have nets here?

Roland   You think you're the first person to think of this? I mean, come on, love, this bridge, Dartford one side, Thurrock on the other, we got people absolutely queuing up.

She peeks over the edge.

Andrea   Where are they meant to be, these nets?

Roland   Right below you, strung all along the frame.

She peeks again. He tiptoes a bit closer.

Andrea   Can't see anything.

Roland   Mmm. Well, you might not, it is dark tonight . . .

She looks back at him, acknowledges his new position.

Andrea   Never seen none before either.

Roland   You'd not be looking out for them before! They're beauties though . . .

Andrea   I have driven over this bridge every day. I would've / noticed . . .

Roland   *Very* fine nets, they are. Fine but strong, truly lovely weaving. The pride of north-west Kent.

She tries to read his expression.

Andrea   Nah . . . nah, you're talking bollocks.

She pulls the scarf back over her mouth.

Roland   Well, I've said my piece, so if you fancy having a crack, then by all means, take your time, I'll just wait here till you're done.

He crunches a nut.

With my cashews.

He crunches another, loudly, making a show of it.

Don't suppose you want one?

She glowers at him.

Didn't think so.

She turns back to the river.

Shame, full of selenium.

She sighs.

Superb for the prostate.

A beat.

Think it's gonna rain soon though, so . . . I know I said 'take your time' and that, but –

Andrea (*muffled*)   Look, can you just –

Roland   What's that?

She pulls the scarf down.

Andrea   Can you like just fuck off? Please? You're really, really fucking annoying.

Roland   You're the one who's on my turf.

Andrea   Only for a few more seconds. And I was kinda hoping that I could –

Roland   Hoping what?

Andrea   Kinda hoping that –

Roland   What?

Andrea   That –

Roland   What?

Andrea   THAT I COULD DO THIS ALONE! OK?! By myself! In silence! I mean, what's it to you, anyway?

Roland   Hey, I was just sitting there in the booth trying to live my life but then you show up, another will-they-won't-they crying on to my bridge –

Andrea   I'm *not* crying.

Roland   – rusting the place up –

Andrea   It's the fucking wind, alright!

Roland   – and blocking off traffic which, frankly, is quite selfish.

Andrea   I'm done with you now.

She covers her ears and turns back out. He takes out his phone, activates the camera and aims it at her.

Roland   Zoom, where's the zoom . . . Ah.

She waves him away. He makes a fake zoom noise. takes a photo. Looks at it.

Roland   Yup. Crying. Not wind tears, those. Don't suppose you fancy taking one of me?

Now deep in concentration, she continues to ignore him. She closes her eyes and shuffles every so slightly towards the edge. She starts to tilt forward.

Roland   *Hypothetically* . . . say there were no nets . . .

Andrea (*snapping back*)   Oh I fucking knew it!

Roland   Hypothetically speaking. If there were no nets . . . what's your technique like?

Andrea   Technique?

Roland   For the dive. Just 'cause if it's halfway decent, you'll go in proper, like a pen, but then you won't drown, you'll just snap right back up, maybe with a broken back to show for it.

Andrea (*holding out the contents of her hand*)   That's what these are for . . .

He looks at the stones dismissively.

Roland   Oh my, you haven't done your research, have you? Look, sod the stones and sod the drowning, with the way the river flows down here it's a right hassle and your body will fight you all the way. What you want to do is flatten out in mid-air so that when you hit the water – SMASH –

He pounds his fist into the flat of his palm. She flinches.

Roland   – it's like concrete. That'll be against your natural instinct, but it's what you've got to do. Now, with a flat shape and a two hundred and thirteen feet drop, you're looking at some serious dismemberment. You know what 'dismemberment' means, yeah? It's not a tickle. But no fuss if you do it that way. Nice and clean.

He awaits a reaction.

Andrea (*mildly traumatised*)   Thanks for the tip.

Roland   But, hey, all of that is only if you clear the nets.

Which you can't. So . . . y'know. 'S all a bit academic.

He pops another cashew. She considers this information.

Andrea   What if you push me?

Roland   Pardon?

Andrea   Yeah . . . Yeah, that'll work. Nice, swift push from a hefty bloke such as yourself. Send me over with a bit of zip, should do the job.

Roland   And why the hell would I do that?

Andrea   I thought you said you wanted to help?

Roland   Yeah, but –

Andrea (*breaking down a little*)   Fucking well help me then, you cunt, instead of –

She shakes. Cold. Vulnerable.

He takes a step closer. She starts to back away.

He raises one hand to placate her, and throws his jacket with the other.

She catches it and slips it on.

He studies her face, notices the bruise.

Roland   Your fella do that to you? That bruise?

Andrea   Are you . . . are you gonna push me or not?

Roland   No way, José.

Andrea   Right then, guess I'll take my chances.

She gets ready to jump.

Roland   OK, OK! Point made, I see you're a determined young lady. How about I recommend you some other bridge? Hey? Plenty of options down the river. I got . . . Hang on.

He fiddles with his phone.

I got a list right here.

He holds the phone out to her. She laughs hollowly.

Roland   What?

Andrea   Nothing, just –

She screws her eyes up.

– can't see it from here.

He takes a couple of steps towards her. He is very close now.

You're alright there, superstar.

She squints tighter as she scans the list. He leads her through it.

Roland   OK, so you got . . . Waterloo, which is kind of a classic, some might say cliché.

Andrea   Pass.

Roland   Tower Bridge'd be a pretty solid shout, though you'll get a lot of passing gawpers, not sure how you'd feel about that.

Andrea   What's that one say? On the end there?

Roland   Ah, that's my wild card, chucking yourself off the Woolwich ferry. Not much glamour, but has a certain local charm.

Andrea   Mmm, think not.

Roland   Personally, I'd go for Barnes. Not too tall, not too busy, water's closer to source and the current's pretty zippy around there, so will drag you right under. Quite picturesque to boot, so plenty to look at on the way down!

He realises he's got into it and checks himself. She considers.

Andrea   Look, sorry, but those are all fucking miles away, car's got nothing in the tank as it is.

Roland   Oh. Right.

Andrea   Really sorry, mate.

He thinks.

Roland   Got enough to make it run?

Andrea   Hey?

Roland   The car. You got enough in the tank to keep it running? For a little while?

Andrea   Should be. Why?

Roland   'Cause you . . . what you could do, right, is you could just come back here, yeah, move your car over to the side, 'cause at the moment it's blocking a lane, and I swear, I swear if you do that, I'll go into my office and find you a nice, long hose to stick in the exhaust. Loop the other end through the back window and hey presto.

Andrea   That works, does it?

Roland   Yup. Better for everyone too.

Andrea   'Cause I had heard that that doesn't always work.

Roland   Yeah no, it does. Proper gentle it is. And you don't have to do nothing either, just turn the engine over, maybe knock on some Beyoncé, drift off. How's that sound?

She waivers.

Roland   Sounds good, don't it?

Andrea   S'pose.

Roland   So what do you say? Deal?

He reaches out for her. A moment passes. It looks like it could happen. But she suddenly sees the purpose on his face and bolts up.

Andrea   Haaah! Hahahahaha, yes, nice try, mate, nice try. You nearly had me there for a sec 'n' all! You're one smooth bastard, you know that?

Roland   Oh fuck you!

Andrea   Smooth, smooth, hose-flogging bastard.

Roland   You want to jump, go ahead and take a leap!

Andrea (*glowing in victory*)   Don't you worry, I'll be off any second now . . .

Roland   Alright, *you* do that, and *I'll* go call the fire department if that's fine by you, give 'em a heads up, 'cause it's a total ballsache getting people out of them nets!

She proudly watches him stomp off. He pauses.

Roland   Oh, and there's usually some sort of penalty slash admin fee. I don't know if you prefer to pay with cash or card or . . . I mean, you've got 20p right here –

Andrea   D'you reckon I'd be out here if I had any sort of money?

Roland   They can do you instalments.

Andrea   Great, bill me from hell.

Roland   Good luck then!

Andrea   And to you!

Roland   I'm really, actually going now!

Andrea   Go on then! So am I!

Roland   Me too!

Andrea   Buh-bye!

He goes. She moves to jump, but stops just before she does. She turns back.

Andrea   Oi! Oi!

Roland (*offstage*)   What now?!

Andrea   You'll be wanting the jacket back, I expect.

He returns.

Roland   No, no, you keep it.

Andrea   Sure?

Roland   Yeah, you'll be needing it – bobbing about down there for a while, I imagine. Bloody freezing, knocked about by the winds and that.

He signals for permission. She hesitates for a moment before allowing him. He climbs out a little on to the girder and looks out.

Still, you'll get a real nice view of daybreak over the estuary. All that smog really brings out the colours, y'know? Wouldn't think flying dirt could look that pretty.

Just watch out for the seagulls. They swoop down and peck at your eyeballs. Nasty.

She winces.

Andrea   Eyeballs?

He realises he's on to something.

Roland   Oh yeah. The love eyeballs, they do.

Andrea   Oh God.

He starts climbing back off.

Roland   One peck is all it takes.

Andrea   Urgh. Stop it.

Roland   One peck'll burst them right apart.

She grimaces. She looks sick.

Andrea   Fuck.

Roland   Horrid.

He savours the moment, satisfied he's changed her mind.

Andrea   Hey, mister . . .

Roland   Yeah?

Andrea   Do you think you can learn to love someone if you try for long enough?

Roland   What?

Andrea   Like if you try really really hard? What'd you reckon? Do you think it could happen?

He is thrown by this. Really thinks about it.

Roland   Doesn't sound worth it to me.

Andrea   Me neither. Thanks.

He turns and goes. She watches him.

Roland (*chirpy*)   So I'll be seeing you in a couple of hours then / will –

She jumps, screaming theatrically.

Roland   Jesus!

A curious thump.

He freezes. He slowly peers over the edge.

Roland   Oh bollocks.

Scene Two

Gone past one a.m. **Roland**'s *office. It's a mess, but the sort of mess that implies a system. It's raining heavily outside.*

Andrea, *eyes closed, slumped in a chair in the middle. The bruise now clearly visible on the side of her face and she is still wearing* **Roland**'s *jacket, as well as a couple of others, over her shoulders.*

A large pile of stones sit on the main table by the window, with others scattered around the pace. Next to the main pile of stones is a stack of dominos. There is a counter with a sink, a sorry-looking microwave and a kettle. A mobile phone and a landline sit on a nearby filing cabinet.

Roland, *dishevelled, an open first-aid kit by his side, is frantically bandaging* **Andrea**'s *leg. There's a lot of bandage – around her leg, over his shoulder, he's making a hash of it.*

Eventually he cuts off the remaining length with some scissors from the kit and ties the bandage off in a massive bunny ears knot. It's dreadful.

Roland   Balls.

He rummages around the office. A flicker of movement from **Andrea**, *but he doesn't see it.*

He finds what he was looking for – a roll of electrical tape. He peels off a length, wraps a length around the bandage and rips it off.

He stands back, and admires his handiwork – he's inordinately proud.

Roland   Back of the net.

He puts the first-aid kit to the side and takes a much-needed second to himself.

Ooh! Er . . .

He rifles through her clothes until he finds her car keys. He walks out of the office.

After a short while, a telephone rings. **Andrea** *stirs.*

From outside, we hear a car start and pull away.

A few moments later, she awakens, drowsily, and checks herself over. She sloughs off most of the jackets.

The phone stops ringing.

Confused, she takes in her surroundings.

She attempts to stand up but immediately recoils in tremendous pain. She winces, pushes her teeth together and tries again, a little slower this time. She screams in pain, drops back in the chair and blacks out.

Roland *re-enters and notices the jackets have fallen off.*

Andrea *seems very still. He checks her pulse and breathing. All OK.*

He sits at his desk. Taps a pen. Stares out of the window. Looks at the crossword on a paper. Already done.

He goes back to tapping the pen. A familiar routine, suddenly less interesting in present 'company'.

He looks at the angle of **Andrea**'s *leg with dissatisfaction. He leans down to readjust it, and as he does she jolts to consciousness, kicking him in the head.*

Roland   / OW!

Andrea   OW!

Roland (*holding his face*)   Ow . . . ah, the princess awak / ens!

Andrea   AAAHHHH!

Roland   Yeah, I have that effect on wom / en.

Andrea   AAAHHHH!

Roland   Calm down, was only checking if you were an organ do / nor.

Andrea   AHHHH!

She is all screamed out but still hyperventilating.

Andrea   Is this it?

Roland   What?

Andrea   I'm . . . Am I . . . Is this . . .

She looks around.

(*Whispers, distraught.*) Is this hell?

He looks around.

Roland   I mean. it gets a little hot in the summer but . . . not hell. Or heaven. You're still on the Dartford Crossing, which I s'pose is somewhere in between!

He laughs at his own joke, nervous. She is a bit lost.

Andrea   So I'm not dead? Feels like I should definitely be dead.

Roland   Definitely not dead. In fact if anything, from the looks of you, I'd say you're basically fine, yeah?

Andrea   Uh . . .

Roland (*unconvincing*)   Yeah. Yeah, you're fine.

Andrea   No . . . hang on, hang on. I drove up . . . through the toll.

Roland   That's right.

Andrea   Got out . . .

Roland   A-star so far.

Andrea   And then I . . . I . . . jumped.

Roland   Close. You drove up, got out, messed me about and *then* jumped, but essentially –

Andrea   I jumped, so why . . . why aren't I . . .

Roland   Oh. Scaffolding.

Andrea   Scaffolding.

Roland   For the painters. Didn't know it was there, they ain't been here in ages. Thought they'd shunted off properly, but seems they just left it all up for whenever they decide to finish the job, the slackers. I swear no one tells anyone anything around here.

Andrea   Painters?

Roland   Yep. Owe your life to lazy workmen.

Andrea   OK. Have you called anyone?

Roland   No point, they won't do anything about it.

Andrea   Not about them, about me.

Roland   Ah, well, the thing is –

Andrea   Come on, come on, police? Ambulance? Flipping Red Arrows? Not fucking hard is it, have you called anyone? You have, haven't you?

Roland   Um no, not yet, but I was planning to –

Andrea   Well. stop planning.

A beat.

Roland   Hey?

Andrea   Stop planning.

Roland   Er, OK . . .

Andrea   Wait, wait, how can I be sure? You might've called 'em already . . . but you're just telling me you haven't!

Roland   Why'd I do that?

Andrea   So . . . so they got time to come before I – In case I – have you –

Roland   No, no, look, I ain't called anyone and I'm not bloody going to. They'd bounce me if they found out I was out there, supposed to ring jumpers in right away and I like having a job, so . . . we're all fine here. With this whole. Arrangement.

Andrea   OK. Good.

Roland   Good.

Andrea   Hang on, did I hear you say you *like* your job?

She is satisfied, more settled.

Andrea   Hold on, what's that on your . . .

Roland   What?

Andrea   On your . . . Oh my God, you've got something massive on your . . . come here a sec.

Roland   What's wrong?

Andrea   Bit closer.

He approaches. She belts him hard across the face.

Roland   Ow! For Christ's sake . . .

Andrea   That's for letting me jump.

Roland   Wouldn't say *let* / exactly –

Andrea   You fucking let me jump!

Roland   I didn't think you were actually gonna do it!

Andrea   Did though, didn't I?!

Roland   And . . . and besides . . . you wanted to, didn't you?

Andrea   Yeah, but like . . .

Roland   So what's your problem, lady?

Andrea   You didn't know that! What if I was some random, mixed-up kid or someone who'd just had a rough day or something, you fucking pyscho!

Roland   You talk to a strange man for a couple minutes, he tells you that jumping off a bridge *won't* kill you and you believe him – who's the psycho?

Andrea   Er, you told me there were nets! Finely woven nets! How was I gonna know? You can't just say that shit to people, people round here are fucking thick.

Roland   Alright . . . sorry.

Andrea   Sorry for?

Roland   For the nets. Happy? There *should* be nets – it's just not very high on the expenditure list. Cheaper to let you drown.

Besides, proves you didn't want to do it after all, don't it. If
Andrea   Hang on, did I hear you say you *like* your job?

She is a bit flatfooted by this. She shrugs.

Andrea   Thought it'd piss you off.

Roland   Oh, that's very mat / ure –

Andrea   Hang on, did I hear you say you *like* your job?

She looks around the room.

This job?

Roland   I said I liked *having* it. Not much else solid going around here.

Andrea   So why'd you bother? Coming out for me?

Roland   Clearly shouldn't have bothered, all the bloody good it's done me.

Andrea   But you did. Could've called it in, could've let me tumble, would've bled out on the scaffolding, with no one but the seagulls the wiser.

He searches around for an answer.

Roland   You were blocking the lanes. Some poor copper doesn't need their tea going cold to sort that just 'cause you've got a flair for the dramatic.

Andrea   Uh-uh . . .

Roland   Speaking of which.

He chucks her car keys to her.

Those are yours, I moved it over.

She pockets the keys.

A thank you would be nice.

Andrea   Thanks, Dad.

Roland   The clutch needs replacing, I reckon.

Andrea   Yeah, I'll get right on that . . .

Using her good leg to propel herself, she tentatively wheels herself towards the table, starts to pick up stones.

Roland   What are you doing?

Andrea   Hm? Oh, I'm heading back out.

Roland   You can't drive like that.

Andrea   I'm not gonna drive, that'd be insane.

Roland   Exactly.

Andrea   Gonna throw myself off again.

Roland   Woah woah woah . . .

He grabs the chair and wheels her back.

I don't think so. I just hauled your arse up here, I'm not getting the ladder out again.

Andrea   Won't have to, I know where the scaffolding is now, don't I?

Roland   No no, no theatrics, what we're gonna do is, you're gonna stay here until . . . let's see . . . a few hours . . .

Andrea   Few hours?!

Roland   Till I clock off and then *I'll* drive you down to Darenth Valley. Tell 'em . . . tell 'em you got kicked by a horse or something.

Andrea   Oh, that's convincing.

Roland   Or decorating, or something, I dunno, you make something up, something that don't involve me. Go to the hospital, I go home, and you can come straight back if you want, I won't tell no one, throw yourself off as many times as you like, couldn't care less. But I'll have done my bit and we can forget this whole thing ever happened.

She thinks it over.

Andrea   Guess that's a slightly better offer than the hose.

Roland   We got a deal then?

Andrea   Alright. Suppose it's nothing that can't wait till morning.

Roland   Perfect. That's settled then.

Andrea   Could quite do with some paracetamol though. You got any paracetamol?

He shakes his head.

Andrea   Come on, I promise I won't chug the lot, just want a couple.

Roland   Haven't got any.

Andrea   You got no painkillers, at all?

Roland   Nope, don't believe in 'em.

Andrea   You don't . . . what do you do when you get a headache?

Roland   Deal with it. Like a man. Some of us don't always take the easy way out.

She rolls her eyes.

Andrea   Something a little stronger then maybe, Mr Manly Man. Must have a little bottle tucked away?

Roland   I don't think so.

She nods her head towards the kettle.

Andrea   Give us a brew then at least?

He looks at her sternly.

Andrea   You *must* have a tea bag.

Roland   Please.

She sighs.

Andrea   Please.

He moves grudgingly towards the kettle. Checks there's enough water in. Flicks it on.

Andrea   Jesus, what are you like.

She drops her head back and closes her eyes.

Roland   Hey hey, you're not meant to sleep if you got . . . if your head is –

Andrea   Myth!

Roland   You what?

Andrea   The thing about concussion and sleeping, that's a myth so just. Leave it.

He sets out two mugs. One he scratches a little stain off, then pops a bag in each.

Situation settled, he relaxes a little. It's all weirdly domestic.

Andrea   By the way, think the phone went while you were out.

He spins.

Roland   What? Which one?

Andrea   Which one?

Roland   Which one?! The landline or the mobile.

Andrea   I dunno. Was just. The phone.

Roland   Was it more of a ddddring or a bbbbbring?

Andrea   Uh, a bbbbbring?

He rushes over to check the mobile. But is disappointed.

Roland   Nothing.

Andrea   Huh. Guess it was a dddddring.

Roland   Great, thanks.

He sulks back to the kettle, which has now boiled, and pours the water out into the cups. He leans against the counter.

So.

Andrea   So.

Roland   Come on then.

Andrea   Come on what?

Roland   Why'd you want to do it? Really.

Andrea   Fuck me, you don't hang around, do you?

Roland   Reasonable question, isn't it? Under the circumstances.

She thinks.

Andrea   Alton Towers ain't open yet.

Roland   Oh, very funny.

Andrea   I know, good one, weren't it.

Roland   Nothing to do with this then?

He pulls out a snapped hospital wrist strap. She opens her eyes.

Andrea   Where'd you get that?

Roland   'Toni Maycock'. That you, is it?

Andrea   How'd you get it?!

Roland   You left it on the dash.

He inspects it.

Roland   Handwriting's a bit faded, can't tell if that's an 'i' or a 'y' on the end. Toni with an 'i'. How Essex are you, exactly?

Andrea   Give it here. It's personal.

Roland   Or is it your fella maybe? Got girly wrists, ain't he. (*Referring to the bruise.*) Surprised he managed to dish that out.

Andrea   That's not yours!

She lunges for it, he steps away. A playful look on his face.

He teasingly holds out the strap. She grabs at it, but he yanks it beyond her grasp.

Roland   Ooh. Nearly.

He holds it out again. She dives for it, smacks him in the nuts. He doubles over. She snatches it away.

Roland (*gasping*)   Fuuuuuuck.

Andrea   Serves you right.

Roland   OK, can we stop with the hitting me, please?

She buries it in her blouse. Composes herself.

Andrea   The money.

Roland   What's that?

Andrea   The money's good. If you kill yourself. Sign up, hold off a few years and it pays out an absolute packet.

Roland You're having me on.

Andrea Nah, seriously, that's the best thing about being young. Fuck up all you want and still have great potential as a life insurance payout.

The phone rings. The mobile. Definitely a bbbbbring. He stares at it dumbly.

Andrea Well, it ain't gonna be for me, is it?

He slowly moves towards the phone and picks it up, almost reverently.

Roland Hello? Oh. Yeah, how you doing boss? Sorry, just didn't think you had this number so I – Uh-uh . . . Right . . . Yes. Well . . . No, no it's fine now. No, nothing to worry about, just stepped out for a smoke. I mean, I was checking the approach for junk, thought I'd seen something come off a lorry and – What I mean is I was smoking while I . . .

No, won't happen again, never again . . . Yeah, I know what'll . . . Hello? Hello? Hello?

He checks the phone. Dead. He chucks it aside.

Roland Sodding phones, batteries get worse every year, don't they? It's how they get you to buy the new ones . . .

Andrea Trouble at the mill?

Roland Nah, just the new supervisor likes to let loose now and then. Not even met the guy yet and he's still giving me grief.

Andrea The supervisor.

Roland Yeah.

Andrea Aren't *you* the supervisor?

Roland I am.

Andrea So how's he the supervisor?

Roland   Everyone's got a boss, don't they? He's the supervisor of me, but I'm the supervisor for this. Section. This . . . arm of the global, you know, operation.

Andrea   Right. Neat. But do you, like –

Roland   Like what?

Andrea   In your position as supervisor, do you like actually supervise anyone?

Roland   Well, I have top-level assets under my responsibility and –

Andrea   Any employees?

Roland   Like a person, you mean?

Andrea   Yeah, being that's what an employee is.

Roland   The traffic flow at this time of night, during my shift, means we don't need – It's complicated.

Andrea   It really ain't. Either you do or you don't.

Roland   No. I don't. But it's still important.

Andrea   So . . . and stop me if I've got this wrong, I'm not exactly the swiftest paedo in the playground . . . Your boss is the supervisor for another supervisor he never sees . . . who supervises no one?

Roland   If you were inclined to look at it through that particular lens –

Andrea   Making you very much the end of the line?

Roland   If you were inclined to look at it through that particular lens . . . I guess that's how it would seem, yeah.

Andrea   Well. Talk about dream careers . . .

Roland   Hah, no such thing! All about working hard and making what you got work for you.

He takes the tea-bags out.

Andrea   Oh, sorry, hadn't realised I'd signed up for a TED talk.

Roland   A what?

Andrea   Never mind.

He gives a cup to her. She scans his name badge.

Andrea   How'd the King of the Supervisors even know you'd gone?

Roland   They got this new thing installed, see, sensors all over, tells him if you've gone away from the office or the booths for too long. Officially it's so they know if you've been kidnapped or beaten up or something, apparently that's a problem, but really it's to make sure you don't disappear. Nobody'd know otherwise. Just me out here with the smog and the machines and they mostly sort themselves out.

Andrea   Blimey. Asda's going that way too, to be fair. Shame, really, could all fuck off down the pub otherwise.

Roland   Yeah.

Andrea   How do you know he's real? The supervisor?

Roland   Of course he's real.

Andrea   Nah, could just be some bloke pretending to be your boss in a call centre miles away. India even.

Roland   He don't sound Indian.

Andrea   Don't mean anything, he could be Indian, could be like six different Indians all using the same English-sounding computer to talk to you. They can do that, they're well crafty over there now.

Roland   Really?

Andrea   Oh yeah, you could just be some dot in a box on a screen, thousand miles away, who they occasionally ring up to give a bollocking to.

Roland   Huh.

Andrea   Or . . . maybe *I'm* your supervisor and this is the world's most elaborate spot check.

She smiles, winks at him and drinks her tea. He smiles a little in spite of himself. Reigns it in.

Roland   Real or not, I should probably –

Andrea   Hey, is your name really Roland?

Roland   What?

Andrea   Your badge. It says.

Roland   Oh.

He examines his badge, as if for the first time.

Roland   . . . Do you not think I can pull off Roland?

Andrea   It's just. You just don't look very much like. Seems a bit. Unlikely. You know? You don't strike me. As a Roland, 'cause you're, y'know, you're . . .

She considers what she's just said.

Is that a bit racist? I'm just being a big old racist, aren't I? Fuck. Fucking minefield, isn't it, all that, these days . . .

A long beat.

Roland   Right. Well, on that bombshell . . . I'm gonna get back to –

Andrea   Andrea. I don't look like one either.

He opens his laptop.

Andrea   No, no, you go right ahead . . .

After an incredibly brief passage of time, she starts trying to peek over his shoulder.

Roland   Do you mind?

Andrea   What?

Roland   Could you . . . go over there or something.

Andrea   Alright . . .

She wheels over to the corner. Stares at the wall. Again, after not too long:

Andrea   Fun, this. Like a sleepover.

She starts swinging her good leg.

Except we always had lots to booze at my sleepovers, you got any booze?

Roland   Already said, not in your state.

Andrea   Pffft.

Roland   What, that a myth too, is it?

Andrea   Nah, just would quite fancy a drink. Don't you fancy a drink?

Roland   Some of us are working here.

Andrea   Are they? I don't see them.

Roland   Well. I am.

Andrea   If you say so . . .

She looks around the sparse office.

I like what you done with the place.

She wheels over to the dominoes, picks one up.

Roland   Leave those alone.

Frustrated, she drops it. He consciously adjusts his screen. He is finding it hard to pretend to be busy.

Andrea   Must be a good place for a cheeky tug this.

That wasn't an offer. I mean, you're alright looking, y'know for an older gentleman and that.

And it's not I've got anything against – you know.

I mean, I dated a Turk once. A Turk, can you imagine! When I was at school.

He was beautiful.

And a bit of a prick actually. Took me horseriding though.
Along the beach. In Southend, of all places.

Southend. Didn't even know they had horses.

Fun.

He turns and looks at her.

Andrea What? For God's sake, no booze, no games, no
reminiscing, what am I meant to do?!

Roland I dunno. Think about what you're doing with your
life maybe.

Andrea That's a good idea, is it?

Roland I'm not your therapist, I've got important –

Andrea Yeah yeah, I heard you the first time, you've got a
game of Solitaire to crack on with.

Roland I'm *not* playing Solitaire.

Andrea Fucking are, I saw you! And you've already
knobbed up the second column when you moved the King
over.

He sighs in frustration.

Roland Look, if I give you something to eat, will you
shut up?

Andrea Depends. What's on the menu?

He goes and opens the fridge.

Roland Your choice of value ready-meals . . . chicken and
mushroom tagliatelle, more chicken and mushroom tagliatelle,
carbonara, macaroni.

Andrea Oooh, an Italian feast . . .

Roland   Oh, and got a Taste the Difference that I usually save for Saturday lunch, or other special occasions but you're welcome to it if you want.

Andrea   Chicken and mushroom'll do me.

He pops it in the microwave. Silence save for the machine buzz.

Roland   Bloody good stuff this. Y'know, for the price.

Andrea   Better be if it's gonna be my last meal.

Roland   Can you. Not.

Andrea   What?

Roland   Do the morbid stuff.

Andrea   Who's morbid? I'm not morbid.

She makes a big, cheery smile.

Roland   You're a kid trying to kill yourself, that's morbid.

Andrea   What, you got to be pushing fifty before it's OK to want to die?

He shakes his head.

Andrea   Sixty? A cripple? A nonce? Terminally ill orphan? What?

Roland   Bloody hell, they don't pay me enough to listen to this.

Andrea *(sing-song)*   I'm not the one with a favourite bridge . . .

The microwave pings.

Roland   Thank fuck!

He serves up the ready-meal, throws the plate in front of her and returns to his 'work'. There's a mood left hanging.

She starts to eat. Screws her face up.

Andrea   'S a bit cold.

He waves away her objections. She picks at the food and then gingerly attempts to shovel it down.

He stares out of the window. Before long she's done with her meal. She pushes the dish away, wipes her mouth with the back of her hand.

Andrea   Heh . . . Roland . . . Roland . . . Roland . . .

Roland (*irritated*)   What?

Andrea   I just thought of something.

She clears her throat.

(*Singing.*) Rolan', Rolan', Rolan' . . . Rolan', Rolan', Rolan'.

He turns from the window.

Andrea (*more purposefully*)   Rolan', Rolan', Rolan' . . .

Roland   What's –

Andrea (*almost tipping off her chair*)   Rolan', Rolan', Rolan', RAWHIDE!

He studies her beaming face.

Roland   The fuck was that?

Andrea   I know, bit of an embarrassment, really.

Roland   No, the song. What was it? Or rather, what's it *meant* to be?

Andrea   *Rawhide.*

Roland   Am I meant to know that?

Andrea   It's some old American show. Cowboys. Had all the videos in Dewhurst. Oh, and that fat guy with the hat sings in it in that movie!

Roland   Dewhurst? I've heard of that, that's . . . is that –

Andrea   The place they keep the naughty ladies, yeah. It's like . . . you ever seen *Bad Girls*?

Roland   No.

Andrea   Liar. Every fella I know's wanked off to *Bad Girls* at some point.

Roland   I haven't. Don't even have a telly, full of shit these days.

Andrea   Uh-uh, methinks the lady doth protest too much.

She starts to wheel herself around the office.

Doesn't matter, actually was nothing like that anyway.

Roland   If you say so.

Andrea   Nothing like that at all.

Roland   I bet.

Andrea   This is where you're meant to ask me what it *was* like.

Roland   I'm not that interested.

Andrea   Yeaaah you are. Everyone always is. Women. Prison.

She whispers.

Lesbo inferno.

Roland   Not me.

Andrea   Go on . . .

He prepares himself a cup of coffee.

Andrea   I've got a cracking line for it. It's the one I use for parties.

Roland   Fine. What was it like?

She halts her wheeling, looks directly at him.

Andrea   Just like a men's prison, but you get to wear a dress while they fuck ya.

She mugs for a laugh that isn't coming.

You are a fucking tough audience, you know that?

Roland I got a kid about your age. He thinks he's funny too. Everything's a joke with your generation, isn't it?

Andrea Ah, everything *is* a joke, old timer, you just don't see it.

Roland Same height, he is . . . Less clever, maybe. Less suicidal, hopefully.

Andrea Mmm, worth checking, that.

Roland Can't. He's gone.

Andrea Gone?

Roland Gone. Doesn't even pick up his bloody phone . . .

Andrea Where's he gone to?

Roland If he picked up I'd know, wouldn't I?

Andrea Been a while then.

Roland Used to ring, but now it just goes straight to answerphone. No point trying any more.

Andrea Can always leave a message.

Roland Want to talk to him, not some tape recorder.

Andrea I'd be surprised if it were a tape recorder . . .

Roland You know what I mean.

Andrea You let anyone know? That he's missing?

Roland He's not missing, he's just a dickhead. Teenagers. You try to point them in the right direction and they snap your finger off for it.

Andrea I see. (*She sips from her tea.*) Take it you've tried Facebook?

Roland Yeah.

Andrea Whatsapp?

Roland No. What's –

He shakes his head.

Andrea   Bebo maybe. That's still big in Scotland, I hear, maybe he's up there . . .

Roland   Look, forget I said anything. I don't know why I –

Andrea   . . . maybe he's sitting in a car with a hose in the exhaust!

He looks at her, disbelieving.

Andrea   What? So I don't get to joke now either?

He fumes.

Oh, don't be mad, come on . . .

She stretches out. She picks up a domino again.

Dominoes? Come on, Mr Soppy Face, teach me. Thought you were all about the life lessons.

He ignores her, goes back to his laptop. She starts chewing on the domino.

Andrea   Fucking hell, that tastes like bear shit.

She throws the domino at him. He slams his laptop shut. The violence surprises her.

Roland   If you're so bored, maybe you should just throw yourself off the bridge? I hear that's a bag of laughs.

She wheels over in her chair, picks up the domino that bounced off him.

Andrea   I hit someone, you know?

Roland   No, really? Would never have guessed.

Andrea   I mean, that's why I was in. I hit a person. A few people actually.

Roland   That gets you a spell now, does it?

Andrea   Depends how hard you hit 'em.

Roland   Well. I'm almost impressed.

And what? Something happened in there that's led you up here? Is that it?

Andrea   That's a theory. Come on, let's do something.

She holds up the domino. Shakes it at him.

Roland   Dunno how you play it properly.

Andrea   Then why the fuck'd you buy 'em?

Roland   I didn't, they were just here, OK? When it gets slow . . . I kinda, y'know, stack 'em up, like that one there. Keep on building till it falls over, and then I build it again, can do it for hours and hours. Heh, although, sometimes, right, sometimes . . . if you get it really big, I mean like you can get it to up *here* if you're careful, then you can play . . . We call it Block Knock and it's where you take the stress ball, stand back by the window and try taking out the tower. Boom! Fifty points if you skittle the lot.

He's worryingly into it.

Thirty for a partial.

It's fun.

Andrea   I take it back. Asda's not this bad.

Roland   See? Always something worse. Not worth doing something drastic about.

Andrea   Yeah, well, my job, though lacking the glamour of the rock-and-roll toll booth lifestyle, isn't what brought me here. Reckon I was in for the sack soon anyway, don't need as many cashiers now they've got the self-service and always easier to can the ex-con first. And once the old birds who can't work the machines are dead – no offence intended – they'll all be gone, I reckon. Poor Janet'll be off down the Odeon to fight it out with some spotty teenager for a job serving nacho cheese to a family of diabetics. If they don't knock it down first.

Roland   Can't fight the future, can you? Ride the wave and all that.

Andrea   And guess you're riding that wave till the very end, huh?

Roland   How'd you mean?

Andrea   'Cause they're shutting the tolls, aren't they?

A long beat.

Roland   What?

Andrea   They said they're ditching them soon. In the paper.

He begins to say something. Stops himself.

Roland   They're . . . Nah, they were talking about it, but they're never actually gonna do it, they'll never get rid of the toll, it's a total cash cow.

Andrea   Not the toll, mean the booths and that, read something about stripping it all out, doing the whole thing with the cameras and the sensors and –

She takes in his face.

Andrea   I assumed you . . . That's why I . . .

Oh. Oh my God, you poor fucker. You didn't know.

Roland   Hang on, who said –

Andrea   Are you kidding me?! You poor, poor fucker!

She laughs hysterically.

Yeah, soon no booths, no barriers, no need for 20p change, no need for people at all. They're just gonna scan your plates and send you a bill. Beep. Beep. Just like at the supermarket.

He is rocked by this news but tries not to show it.

Andrea   Guess they didn't include you in the consultation then?

Roland   They're still gonna need a person – in case it – I mean, they'll still need someone to sort it when the machines cock up so –

Andrea   Yeah, maybe, but it'll be someone who knows computers in a real office somewhere, not some right thicko like you strung out in this shithole.

She laughs. He isn't smiling any more.

Andrea   Aw, don't get too upset. If you stick about to the bitter end they might give you a pat on the head. Or you could spite your Indian overlords and take a tumble like me. We could go together! Like a synchronised dive team.

He is rigid.

Roland   I don't think I have the figure.

Andrea   In this light, you could probably get away with it.

A beat. She realises she's gone a bit far.

Andrea   Erm . . . well . . . if we're not gonna kill ourselves, if we're not gonna do that just yet then . . . hmm . . . you got wifi here?

He nods.

Andrea   Right then. I know just what you need.

Scene Three

Four a.m. **Roland** *and* **Andrea** *sit side by side.*

Roland*, wearing a pair of in-ear headphones, stares intently at the laptop, absolutely rapt.*

Andrea*, haphazardly wrapped all over in bandages like a half-cut mummy, reads a logbook, occasionally casting an eye over the screen.*

They are in the middle of a trashy TV marathon.

Roland   Who knew that Newcastle even *had* a shore?

A variety of expressions pass between the two of them.

Roland   Can't get over those tans, it's like staring at the sun.

She looks perplexed.

Andrea   Roland? Hey, Roland?

Roland (*distracted*)   Yuh-huh?

Andrea   Why's this one got a question mark by it?

He takes out the headphone.

Roland   What's that?

Andrea   I said, why's this one got a question mark? 'Incident. November 06.'

Roland   Oh. Him. Don't know what happened with him.

Andrea   You can take a good guess.

Roland   No, I mean, usually there's a report, an article after. On that guy, nothing.

Andrea   Huh. You know, you don't actually have any bungee jumpers in here.

Roland   Yeah, well. Hope springs.

He sticks his headphones back in. They go back to their activities. He almost immediately pulls the headphones back out.

Roland   Wait, hold on, hold on, which one's that? Have we had him before?

Andrea   Who?

Roland   He's gone now. The one with the mullet and the lacy tank-top. There! Is that Sebastian?

Andrea   Oh no, that's Kev-Kev.

Roland   They all look the same!

Andrea   Now who's a racist?

Roland   They do though!

Andrea   Nah-nah, look, Sebastian's new, got a stud in the right ear, Kev-Kev was in the first season, has a hoop in the left.

Roland   OK.

Andrea   He's the one seeing Amy.

Roland   Ah . . . but maybe he's also the guy we've heard about . . . who's nailing Jennie?

Andrea   That's it, you're catching on, and poor Amy, oh, poor poor Amy –

Roland   Poor Amy doesn't know?

Andrea   Exactly. And Jennie is actually Amy's sister-in-law from her second marriage, which *they* both know of course but Kev-Kev doesn't.

He takes this in.

Roland   Christ on a bike. And what about . . .

She gives him a knowing look.

Roland   . . . No!

Andrea   Uh-huh.

Roland   Sebastian . . . was the second husband!

Andrea   Bingo. You are good at this, you are.

Roland   That's messed up.

Andrea   Ain't it though.

Roland   I can't believe it.

Andrea   Intense, right?

Roland   No, I can't believe this is what I'm doing with my time.

Andrea   Well . . . imagine this or cowboys, but for five years. That was prison, that was the real punishment.

Roland   Bloody hate that, I would. Being locked up.

Andrea   'S not so bad, there's a lovely certainty to it.
Regular hours, no shirty customers, no three a.m. stocktakes.
Nobody wanting to replace you with a barcode scanner.

He snorts in agreement.

Roland   Can we try the one with the cowboys?

Andrea   *Rawhide?*

Roland   Yeah. I like the idea of that. If I watch any more
of this one I think I'll top myse –

He cuts himself off. She acknowledges it with a smirk.

Andrea   Yeah, I'm sure I can find it somewhere. Hang on.

*She wheels herself closer and starts fiddling with the laptop. He looks out
of the window. He starts waving an arm up and down.*

Andrea (*not taking her eyes off the screen*)   What. The fuck. Are
you doing?

Roland   Waving. At the booths. First people starting to go
through now, always looks like the barriers are waving at you
from here. Up. Down. Up. Down. Heh.

She shakes her head.

Andrea (*under her breath*)   Oh my days.

He turns back to her.

Roland   You know, it is nice. Talking to someone, an adult.
Properly. Makes a change.

Andrea   Yeah?

Roland   Sure. I've been having the same ten-second
conversation for the last decade.

Andrea   That all people can take of you before they jump,
is it?

Roland   Hah, nah, meant the drivers. The jumpers, they . . .
all the people in that book, never got a chance to talk to any
of them. I just make the call and then I watch them looking
down. Rolling the thought over in their minds. 'Is it really all
that bad?'

Andrea   'Maybe I should go have a Nando's at Bluewater
and calm down.'

Roland   Exactly. Then the police come, push past and
spend two hours trying to talk them down.

And they jump anyway. Every time I've been here. Same
thing over and over, I see 'em through the window, every
single one, these little black darts slipping through the lights
and vanishing into the river.

You can hear the splash from here.

He is on the verge of cracking.

Andrea (*making light*)   So what, I was your first? I popped
your suicidal cherry?

Roland   I guess . . .

Andrea (*melodramatic*)   But Roland, you seemed so
experienced, you had your patter all figured out and
everything.

Roland   As you say, got a lot of time on my hands.

Andrea   Well. That's . . . I'm honoured.

She smiles.

I know it looks like I'm taking the piss, I'm not, I am touched.
Truly.

It's a lovely moment.

But I also really need to go for a wazz, so . . .

*She wheels out a little from the laptop and attempts to stand. He watches
her, tense. She just about manages it, but needs the chair for support.*

Roland   Whey!

Andrea   Whey! That, my friend, is the healing power of telly. Who needs Jesus when you've got box sets?

She wheels the chair away, unsteadily, and exits. He turns back to the laptop. Clicks to start something playing.

Andrea *can be heard peeing. Perturbed,* **Roland** *puts both the headphones in and bumps up the volume.*

He laughs loudly at the screen. He shakes his head.

Roland (*to himself*)   That man is *not* from Honduras.

Andrea *returns.* **Roland** *watches on, oblivious as she observes him.*

He laughs again, raucously. She smiles as she takes in his joy.

She turns to stare out of the window. Her smile half drops.

Andrea   Gonna be getting light soon.

He hears and spins on his chair.

Roland   D'you say something?

Andrea   Um, I said your toilet's very clean for a bloke, I'm impressed. Not a pube or piss-splash in sight.

Roland   Thanks.

He registers her change in mood.

Can I get you something?

Andrea   Nah.

Roland   Maybe you should sit . . .

Andrea   Nah nah, it's fine, nothing wrong with – Oh oh, don't miss this bit, this bit's amazing.

He returns to the screen. She looks out at the bridge. He chuckles, shakes his head, slumps back into watching.

She has a moment of absolute clarity. She makes a decision.

Andrea   Hey, actually, Roland, could you do me a favour?

Roland   What's up?

Andrea   I – I know this'll sound really dumb, but I left my nail file in the car, yeah, and these babies are . . . they're all over the fucking place.

She presents her nails to him.

Roland   Look alright to me.

Andrea   Oh mate, no, see there? Loads of little chips, it's really stressing me out. Urgh. Can't stop looking at 'em. Embarrassing, really. Gotta have standards, don't you?

Roland   You're not exactly at the Ritz, I wouldn't worry.

Andrea   Still, bugs me. Will you go and get the file for us?

Roland (*uncertain*)   I dunno. Can't you just . . .

He scans the office.

Do it on one of the rocks?

Andrea   With cuticles this good? Don't be a fucking monster, Roland.

He stares at her, suspicious.

Would make me feel better, yeah? Doing my nails.

He doesn't move.

You can lock me in for all I care, but if I'm going to be sticking about after all, would help to do something normal.

He is satisfied.

Roland   Alright. Your Majesty.

He holds out his hands for the keys. She chucks them to him.

He leaves, casting one eye back at her, but without locking the door. She examines her nails.

Once he is out of the door, she springs into action. She starts gathering stones. Needing the chair for support, it's a painfully slow process. Midway, she pauses. A thought.

She wheels over to the phone, picks up and referencing a document besides it, dials a number. It rings for a long while. She eyes the door, nervously.

Andrea   Hi! Yeah, I'm calling on behalf of Roland, er . . . Roland . . . just Roland. You know who I mean, yeah? Yeah, he says to let you know . . . He just wanted to let you know that he thinks that you're a lying cunt and possibly a robot. Cheers.

She hangs up and goes back to collecting stones.

After a few moments, **Roland** *re-enters.*

He looks up and sees **Andrea** *pocketing the stones. He watches her in silence.*

Roland   Want a hand?

She rises.

Andrea   I was just. Collecting them together. So we could do a game.

Roland   A game.

Andrea   Yeah, a new one. Got to get them in the bin from back there.

She pulls some stones from her pockets and offers them to him.

He does not take them. She presses them into his hand.

My rules though, so none of this partial nonsense, if you get it in, you win big.

He stares at her.

Andrea   Sounds a bit dirty, that.

She forces a chuckle.

Obviously, I'll give you a head start.

He turns and locks the door.

Andrea   Roland, wait a –

Roland   Sit down.

Andrea   You don't –

Roland   SIT. DOWN.

She sits, slowly.

You said you'd stay.

Andrea   I –

Roland   Stay a few hours, that's what you said.

Andrea   I have stayed. Gonna be morning soon. Remember *that* part of the deal?

Roland   Don't care, deal's off, I'm not letting you.

Andrea   Roland . . .

Roland   I'm not.

Andrea   Roland, listen / to –

Roland   There's something better out there for you than this.

Andrea   Better death, maybe, better life, I doubt.

Roland   Oh stop it.

Andrea   Stop what?

Roland   It's boring now. All this . . . You don't even want to do it, yeah? Not really. You were shaking, I saw you.

Andrea   It was cold.

Roland   I know this game, you were up there waiting, just waiting for some chump like me to notice you. That's why they never jump right away.

Andrea   Hah . . .

Roland   Yeah, that's all you're after, isn't it? Spent a few years out of sight, it fucked you up and now you want people to look. Look at you again, pay attention, as many people as you can get. That's all this is. No wonder he fucking hit you.

How vain. How vain you are! Here.

He reaches into his pocket, pulls out his wallet, throws money at her.

Here, that's for a therapist, go sort your shit out, you fucking attention-seeking . . . fucking . . .

He runs out of steam. A long pause.

She smiles at him, bemused, but there's something sinister in it.

Andrea   I'll tell you something, shall I . . .

She wheels over to the dominoes and starts to build a domino tower.

Roland   Shut up now.

Andrea   You'll get a real kick out of this, I tell / you.

Roland   I told you to / shut –

Andrea   No, listen! You need to fucking listen to me, Roland, listen to someone else for once, yeah? I'm not looking for your money, or your attention. I have just calmly accepted, like an adult, that I don't want to teeter along no more, hoping that it's all going to get better.

I've done the therapy, done the pills, done all of that inside, that didn't fuck me up, they tried to help. They try to get you to make little changes, little things to get you by. Routines. Tricks. But they aren't enough, it's too little paint over too many cracks. It's bigger than that, something big in here, something has gone totally wrong. No, was always wrong, and it's not the kinda thing that feels like you can get fixed.

He attempts to speak, but she cuts him off, while delicately placing a domino on the increasingly tall tower.

Andrea   Yeah, you get good days. Where everything is great. Where you want to live your life for other people, give them everything – stop being some mopey, selfish bitch. You even get it into your head that maybe there's a chance you can change, be alright, that you can solve everything before bedtime.

But you still wake up broken the next morning, and that's not living, that's coping, and, Mr Roland, I am so very, very tired of coping. It's the worst kind of existence.

But look, it's alright, all of that doesn't matter, yeah, 'cause here's the wonderful thing, the really most wonderful thing. When I made a decision, when I jumped. It was this incredible sensation . . . It was bliss.

Roland   Bliss? Fuck off. You were scared.

Andrea   Course I was scared, standing on the side of a bridge is still fucking scary and I think in the end I *did* jump to spite you, but once I done it, all the rest of it, all the fear, all the doubt, that all dropped away and in those seconds I was falling there was just this joy, this utter holy bliss.

He is in deep thought. This has struck a chord.

She casually lobs the stress ball at the tower. It misses.

Andrea (*grimly cheerful*)   Ah tits. (*She looks out.*) I should do it before it gets too busy.

Roland   Look . . . I'll take you home, I said I'd take you, just gimme another hour . . .

Andrea   Rather not hang around, mate.

Roland   A bloody cab then! I'll just charge my phone up and –

Andrea   No no, no need to be extravagant on my behalf . . .

Roland   Fuck it, OK then, now. Let's go now. Right.

Andrea   Aren't you forgetting . . .

Roland   . . . the sensors.

Andrea   The sensors, right. Luckily, I have a solution that sorts both our problems.

Roland   Gonna make me get the guys with the straitjackets, is that it?

Andrea   You know I'll still do it, right? If not here, then somewhere, if not now, later, I'll find a way, you can't stop me.

She starts to wheel away. He grabs her arm.

Roland   I could.

Andrea   I would scream so loud, for so long / you

Roland   To who? The oil depot? The container ships? The eye-pecking seagulls? There's no one around here. There's never no one around here, 'cept for people like me!

Andrea   And people like me.

Roland   Yeah, well, the people like you don't tend to hang around very long, do you? Talk to the police and then fuck off into the river!

He pulls her back, she tries to shove him away. They struggle. She can't break his grip.

Andrea   You're a useless cunt, you know that.

Roland   Hah, that's not going to work, I'm afraid.

Andrea   Oh you're afraid? You know what I'm still afraid of? More than being trapped in this hell-hole, more than death, more than absolutely anything else ever? I'm afraid my son will end up just like you.

Roland   Son?

Andrea   Tony ain't my boyfriend, Roland, he's my boy. And you are the worst thing I can imagine happening to him, I would literally rather he ended up on the dole for life, a washed-up, no-hoper than some judgemental piece of shit like you that can't figure out that he don't mean nothing to no one!

She tries to rise and he, angered, pushes her down, hard. She tumbles backwards on to the floor and screams in pain.

Roland   Oh Christ! I'm so . . .

She lies on the floor, breathing sharply in shock. He rushes in to help.

Andrea   NO!

Startled, he halts. A moment later he starts to edge forward again but she raises her palm to stop him.

After a moment, she begins to rise – slowly: knee first, a muscle at a time. It is excruciatingly slow, and she is clearly in agony, but she manages it. She stretches upright and holds her position, unassisted, with a regal dignity.

It is a moment of wonder. She catches her breath. She can't quite believe it.

Andrea (*brushing herself off*)   See, in my experience, the trick is to hit 'em so that they don't get up again.

She shuffles along, tentatively. He watches her with awe.

He notices she's dropped the hospital strap. He picks it up.

Roland   Here, you dropped . . . your . . .

She takes the strap. Stares at it.

Andrea   Heh. Had him when I was inside, they wouldn't let me keep him, Dad's fucked off of course, so it was Mum or a home. And well . . . she loved that, having another roll of the dice.

All I looked forward to my whole time inside was making him safe, making him happy, squeezing him till his little eyes popped out.

He was there when I walked through the gate, waiting in the car like an angel, just like the pictures she sent me. He wouldn't get out, though, so I had to lean myself over, got my arms half around him, half tangled in the seat belt. I squeezed.

And he bloody hated it. Looked at me like I'd just tucked my hands down his pants or something.

No worries, I figured it'd take a little time, a little effort, so when I got back I made him his favourite, right . . . meatballs and mash, the exact recipe his gran makes him, but he didn't like it. Sulked for two hours that I'd done it wrong. Identical.

Just 'cause she didn't make it. Cow. Tried for months and months and then . . . well, soon he wouldn't even look at me, would act like I weren't there. So this morning I try and *make* him look.

Worse idea than it sounds. He just whacks me in the face and runs off to Gran. Hard hands for a five-year-old, I'll give him that.

Roland   Kids, they're – sometimes they'll be like that, you just gotta –

Andrea   I wanted to hit him back, you understand? Bash his little face right in. Crush his skull, rip his fucking nose off. I saw myself doing it in my mind, and I realised . . . he's already safe, already happy . . . and between my pay-out and her pension, he'll be able to do whatever the fuck he dreams of which is better than most around here.

And yeah, I could be working day after shitty day, surviving to work *another* shitty day, hoping it might be a good one, hoping to make the best of it, hoping to find some other justification for my air sucking, while the bills stack up and my parts drop off.

Or I get bliss. He gets a life. I done enough, the rest is just . . . noise.

She thinks.

I was here, I lived, I loved, I did, I've done, everything that I wanted.

A beat.

Roland   That's Beyoncé.

Andrea   Yeah. Thought you'd appreciate . . .

He nods slowly. Hobbling, she starts to collect her things.

Roland   Look, Andrea, I get it, believe me I do, I get it more than you know, just that – and I'm not suggesting that like . . . I've come to love you or nothing, you really wind me up actually and I don't know you from Adam and this'll sound really weird, just.

I think if you go out there it might just break my heart.

She is halted by that. She turns to him.

Andrea   Not quite Nando's at Bluewater, but if there's nothing else that's gonna keep you from . . . from . . .

He can't bring himself to say it. She looks right into him. He's serious. She wobbles a little. A real hint that she might reconsider.

Andrea   Oh . . . you daft soppy cunt. You don't mean that.

Roland   I do. I know it can't be worth much to you but I –

She cuts him off with a tight hug. It's important to them both, the first proper hug either has had in years, and takes as long as it needs to.

Roland (*muffled*)   Sorry.

Andrea   It's OK.

Roland   No, for the BO.

Andrea   Oh. No worries, I'm worse, got a lot of layers going on here.

They hold on a bit longer. She pulls out of the hug and looks at him.

You did better than the pros, you know that? I'd have been long off the deep end by now if you called the cops. *You* should go pro.

She considers.

Well, your technique would need finessing . . .

But if you're itching for a job with slightly less suicides to deal with, there's about to be an opening at Asda.

He laughs, very weakly, but he is out of the moment. She returns to her task. He understands something about himself.

Roland   I've . . . I've always hoped that . . . when they do it. That somehow it's for the best.

He picks up some stones. Offers them to her.

Sure I got something heavier around the back if you fancy it.

She looks at the stones.

Andrea   You know what? Fuck it, no point wasting a good coat.

She takes off her coat, places it aside. And then her cardigan. It turns out she is wearing quite a nice dress. He whistles in admiration.

Andrea   Thanks. George Collection. Think Myleen designed it.

Roland   Could probably still find you that hose . . .

Andrea   Heh, it's fine.

Roland   Or. That push maybe.

Andrea (*warmly*)   It's fine, Roland.

Roland   Just trying to help.

Andrea   Yeah, I know. Flat out, right? Not a pen.

Roland   Right. Like you're flying. There's the dismemberment but like . . . in the scheme of things that's –

Andrea   Just a tickle.

She makes for the door. He is utterly dejected.

Andrea   Best of luck with it all though, yeah? I'm sure . . . what's his name, your kid?

Roland   Ade.

Andrea   I'm sure Ade's alright.

Roland (*as she walks away*)   Will you drink to that?

He slowly pulls some whisky out of a hiding place.

Call it a penalty fee.

She considers.

Roland   It's Tesco's Finest.

She smiles.

Andrea   Go on then. One for the road.

Scene Four

Morning. **Roland**'s *flat. Cramped, junk is scattered all around.*
Roland *enters, swaying, a little jolly perhaps, as if after a night out.*

He is wearing his jacket and carries carrier bags full of items from the office.

He stumbles and knocks his thigh into the telephone table.

Roland   Ugh. For fuck's sake . . .

*His jolliness dissipates. Shoving the table out of the way, he dumps
the bags.*

*He reaches into the pockets of his coat and pulls out a ready-meal. The
Taste the Difference. He looks at it longingly and pops it into the
microwave.*

While it cooks, he wanders to the table and sits, heavily.

*Exhaustion slowly begins to creep over him. He looks like he's about to
bawl his eyes out.*

*The phone rings. He reaches back on his chair – a perilous exercise – and
just about gets it without falling.*

Roland   Heeey there. How's it going, boss? Oh yeah, yeah,
they don't show anyone there 'cause I'm not there . . . What?
. . . No, I – I never asked anyone to do that. Wouldn't of said
that, that must've been . . . heh.

The microwave bings.

Oh! Give us a sec, boss.

*He retrieves his ready-meal and dishes it up, humming a snatch of a song
as he goes. The phone squawks as he does. He returns, eating as talks.
His tone is casual throughout.*

OK, go. No, I ain't sick, just – Uhuh. Uhuh. No . . . No . . .
I . . . ahhh you know what, you know what, you can't sack
me, you can't sack me 'cause I was quitting anyway so fuck
off, do fuck off. Do. Just. Fuck. Off.

He begins to puts the phone down when a thought occurs to him.

Wait wait, hold on, hold on! Sorry, sorry, there's something
I've gotta ask, I've gotta . . .

A beat.

Are you some bloke on a computer in India? Bet the
weather's well nice.

He listens to the reply.

Oh. Colchester? Unlucky.

Satisfied, he hangs up. He takes a few more bites of his meal.

He stops. He makes a decision.

*He reaches back to the phone, grabs the handset and dials a number. He
pulls something out of his pocket – one of the stones. No answer on the
phone, the barely audible rabbiting of an answerphone followed by a beep.*

So. It's me. Leaving a message. As requested. Not ideal but –

*This is unpleasant. He fiddles with the stone. He has the briefest flit of
second thoughts but he rallies with a burst.*

But I mean if you won't pick up, if you ain't ever gonna pick
up, I guess I'm just gonna talk to you anyways, you prick, you
fucking selfish little prick!

He flings the stone across the room.

You don't get away from me that easily!

The rage subsides.

Sorry . . . sorry, I didn't mean that. I just –

He gives up.

Just wanted to tell you about my day.

From here on in, he wanders about, tidying the place.

I met a girl. On the bridge of all places, if you can believe that. She was about your age, I reckon. Maybe a bit older. You both got a mouth on you, so you'd approve.

We met, got chatting about this and that, I bring her back to mine, heh . . . Nah, nah, it weren't like that, your old man ain't that kinda dog. Though she did tell me that I had nice eyebrows, which is exactly what your mum said to me the first time I took her out.

Anyway, she was laughing, I was laughing if you can believe that, going pretty well all things considered. Even had one or two drinks and played a bit of that game you invented with the dominoes, bit of a party in the end actually.

But then she says she's got to be off, she's got this thing she has to do. I beg her to stay a bit longer, but nothing doing, she really wants to get it done, so I let her go. And on her way up she's singing this song, from that cowboy show . . .

He sings, slow, clear and haunting.

Rolan' Rolan' Rolan' . . . Rolan' Rolan' Rolan' . . . Rolan' Rolan' Rolan' . . .

He breaks from singing.

Rawhide. It's pretty old, I don't know if you'd know it. As she gets to the top of the road deck she looks back to me and she starts to wave and I pull the blinds down. This one I don't want to see.

And I don't know why, I think I've gone a bit crazy, or maybe the drink got to me quick but I nearly, I so nearly – all I want in the world just then is to run up there, step out on that girder with her and I . . .

He finds the stone he chucked earlier. It makes him smile.

Ade, I know if you were here now, you'd be standing by the sofa, pointing two fingers at me with fury like you do, screaming 'You let her go?! That was a fucking stupid thing to do, Dad!' and hey, that might be true, but it just felt right to me. In the moment. Felt like the best thing I'd ever done for anyone.

He walks to the window and peers down the street.

I watched the water till the sun came up. Took a while, but it's worth it. You get some wonderful sunrises climbing out of that river, all just for you.

Boy – I don't know where you are. Don't know what you're doing, don't know what you've done. You could be on top of a mountain or under the ocean, somewhere over the fucking rainbow maybe or . . . or even just down the road, I dunno.

But whatever you're up to, I hope you least got someone there with you, seeing you through.

He lets the handset slip. Relief. He considers the stone in his hand.

Y'know, I didn't hear a splash.

Lights down.

 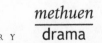

Bloomsbury Methuen Drama Modern Plays

include work by

Bola Agbaje	Robert Holman
Edward Albee	Caroline Horton
Davey Anderson	Terry Johnson
Jean Anouilh	Sarah Kane
John Arden	Barrie Keeffe
Peter Barnes	Doug Lucie
Sebastian Barry	Anders Lustgarten
Alistair Beaton	David Mamet
Brendan Behan	Patrick Marber
Edward Bond	Martin McDonagh
William Boyd	Arthur Miller
Bertolt Brecht	D. C. Moore
Howard Brenton	Tom Murphy
Amelia Bullmore	Phyllis Nagy
Anthony Burgess	Anthony Neilson
Leo Butler	Peter Nichols
Jim Cartwright	Joe Orton
Lolita Chakrabarti	Joe Penhall
Caryl Churchill	Luigi Pirandello
Lucinda Coxon	Stephen Poliakoff
Curious Directive	Lucy Prebble
Nick Darke	Peter Quilter
Shelagh Delaney	Mark Ravenhill
Ishy Din	Philip Ridley
Claire Dowie	Willy Russell
David Edgar	Jean-Paul Sartre
David Eldridge	Sam Shepard
Dario Fo	Martin Sherman
Michael Frayn	Wole Soyinka
John Godber	Simon Stephens
Paul Godfrey	Peter Straughan
James Graham	Kate Tempest
David Greig	Theatre Workshop
John Guare	Judy Upton
Mark Haddon	Timberlake Wertenbaker
Peter Handke	Roy Williams
David Harrower	Snoo Wilson
Jonathan Harvey	Frances Ya-Chu Cowhig
Iain Heggie	Benjamin Zephaniah

Bloomsbury Methuen Drama Student Editions

Jean Anouilh *Antigone* • John Arden *Serjeant Musgrave's Dance* • Alan Ayckbourn *Confusions* • Aphra Behn *The Rover* • Edward Bond *Lear* • *Saved* • Bertolt Brecht *The Caucasian Chalk Circle* • *Fear and Misery in the Third Reich* • *The Good Person of Szechwan* • *Life of Galileo* • *Mother Courage and Her Children* • *The Resistible Rise of Arturo Ui* • *The Threepenny Opera* • Anton Chekhov *The Cherry Orchard* • *The Seagull* • *Three Sisters* • *Uncle Vanya* • Caryl Churchill *Serious Money* • *Top Girls* • Shelagh Delaney *A Taste of Honey* • Euripides *Elektra* • *Medea* • Dario Fo *Accidental Death of an Anarchist* • Michael Frayn *Copenhagen* • John Galsworthy *Strife* • Nikolai Gogol *The Government Inspector* • Carlo Goldoni *A Servant to Two Masters* • Lorraine Hansberry *A Raisin in the Sun* • Robert Holman *Across Oka* • Henrik Ibsen *A Doll's House* • *Ghosts* • *Hedda Gabler* • Sarah Kane *4.48 Psychosis* • *Blasted* • Charlotte Keatley *My Mother Said I Never Should* • Bernard Kops *Dreams of Anne Frank* • Federico García Lorca *Blood Wedding* • *Doña Rosita the Spinster* (bilingual edition) • *The House of Bernarda Alba* (bilingual edition) • *Yerma* (bilingual edition) • David Mamet *Glengarry Glen Ross* • *Oleanna* • Patrick Marber *Closer* • John Marston *The Malcontent* • Martin McDonagh *The Lieutenant of Inishmore* • *The Lonesome West* • *The Beauty Queen of Leenane* • Arthur Miller *All My Sons* • *The Crucible* • *A View from the Bridge* • *Death of a Salesman* • *The Price* • *After the Fall* • *The Last Yankee* • *A Memory of Two Mondays* • *Broken Glass* • Joe Orton *Loot* • Joe Penhall *Blue/Orange* • Luigi Pirandello *Six Characters in Search of an Author* • Lucy Prebble *Enron* • Mark Ravenhill *Shopping and F***ing* • Willy Russell *Blood Brothers* • *Educating Rita* • Sophocles *Antigone* • *Oedipus the King* • Wole Soyinka *Death and the King's Horseman* • Shelagh Stephenson *The Memory of Water* • August Strindberg *Miss Julie* • J. M. Synge *The Playboy of the Western World* • Theatre Workshop *Oh What a Lovely War* • Frank Wedekind *Spring Awakening* • Timberlake Wertenbaker *Our Country's Good* • Arnold Wesker *The Merchant* • Oscar Wilde *The Importance of Being Earnest* • Tennessee Williams *A Streetcar Named Desire* • *The Glass Menagerie* • *Cat on a Hot Tin Roof* • *Sweet Bird of Youth*

For a complete listing of Bloomsbury
Methuen Drama titles, visit:
www.bloomsbury.com/drama

Follow us on Twitter and keep up to date
with our news and publications
@MethuenDrama